The really, really, really useful Guide Number 10

CLINGERS, CREEPERS AND SCRAMBLERS

What kind of climber are you?

MIKE PEARCE

Copyright 2017 by Mike Pearce

All rights reserved. No part of this book may be reproduced, distributed or transmitted in any form or by any means, including photocopying, recording, or other electronic or mechanical methods, without the prior written permission of the author, except in the case of brief quotations embodied in reviews and certain other non-commercial uses permitted by copyright law. You must not circulate this book in any format.

This book may not be resold or given away to other people. Please respect the work of the author and purchase a copy for your own use.

To see other publications by the author visit snappysnappybooks.com

Copyright © 2017 Mike Pearce

All rights reserved.

ISBN:10:197656591X
ISBN-13:978-1976565915

DEDICATION

This book is dedicated to those people trying to get a hold in life in order to build up a business or succeed in whatever they do

CONTENTS

Acknowledgements
Preface

1	Are you a creeper or a scrambler?	1
2	Are you a climber or revolver?	3
3	Are you a clinger or a climber?	6
4	Are you a twiner using tendrils for attachments?	8
5	Are you a twiner using external parts to make contact?	11
6	Some advice for prospective climbers	12

ACKNOWLEDGEMENTS

The author would like to thank Christine Pearce for
reading and checking the manuscript

PREFACE

They had no money. Jack traded his cow for a handful of dried up beans. His mother screamed that he'd been cheated and they were ruined and took hold of the beans and threw them out of the window. The next morning his bedroom was filled with a pale green light as the sun shone through. Green hand like leaves pressed against his window. He went outside with his mother and saw that the beans had grown and their stalks were thick and spiraled around each other running up into the sky as if reaching up through the clouds to reach the sun. Jack climbed up the twining stems and found his fortune and after cutting down the beanstalk with an axe and killing the giant was able to live in luxury throughout his life.

Some plants like beans grow quicker than others moving their modified stems, leaves and roots to find the best situation for their existence. The climbing, twining bean stalk led to Jack's success. Plants, especially climbers, have learnt how to be successful and satisfy their needs. Even Charles Darwin was fascinated by the diverse ways families of plants could move and attach themselves to their surroundings and wrote several essays on them. Families of climbers are found in Begoniaceae, Vitaceae, Leguminosae, Menispermaceae, Passifloraceae, Calamoideae and Convolvulaceae.

This book gives you some examples of how plants struggle to get to the top to maximise their potential and produce flowers and fruits. By adapting one or several of these methods through your life you too can be successful like these plants and reach the top of the beanstalk to gain wealth and happiness but always watch out for giants.

See also How to be a Successful Business Weed

See snappysnappybooks.com for a wide range of self-help fiction and non-fiction books

MIKE PEARCE

From Misalliance -Flanders and Swann

The fragrant honeysuckle spirals clockwise to the sun,

And many other creepers do the same.

But some climb ant-clockwise, the bindweed does, for one,

Or convolvulus, to give her proper name.

Rooted on either side a door, one of each species grew,

And raced towards the window-ledge above.

Each corkscrewed to the lintel in the only way it knew,

Where they stopped, touched tendrils, smiled and fell in love.

"It seems they're against us, all fate has combined. Oh my darling, oh my darling, oh my darling Columbine,
Thou art lost and gone forever, we shall never intertwine".

1 ARE YOU A CREEPER AND SCRAMBLER?

Do you never really get very high but with support you know you can reach great heights?

Do you have the ability to scramble like a bramble, aimlessly hooking with backward facing spines onto things as your interest grows or have lots of small interests which help you creep forward? You proceed on a vertical path forwards but can clamber over things on the way and are readily eager to accept support to raise you higher.

Perhaps, like some plants, you aim for dark places where there is not much activity and know there are individuals like the base of tree that will support you to a point so as to help you to go straight up. A blackberry can extend as much as three inches a day. Can you move forward that fast? There is a need to look for small opportunities as these can have big payoffs. In your effort to get to the top quickly you might try to take short cuts, but this could lead to losing valuable time by making mistakes.

MIKE PEARCE

Cultivate the knack of spotting opportunities where others can only see problems. Look for gaps in the market to become more productive.

2 ARE YOU A CLIMBER OR REVOLVER?

Do you circle around things that interest you trying and trying to get a firm hold?

You are ready to twine around things to get higher but in some cases still need support, like a clematis and wisteria. If you expand your territory too much, grow too big you can tumble back down to the ground but can always change direction as you travel. Twining in most cases turns to the right e.g. Wisteria.

You need to take care not to loosely link to your new support as you may slip down. Twine around others also working in this way so you can support each other. Many have someone to help them and avoid the mistakes that could stop them from getting to the top.

As you travel upwards you can, like plants, achieve more strength from your initial efforts.

As you wind your way upwards you may circumnutate i.e. revolve like a bindweed looking for opportunities in every direction to latch and hook onto. If you fail to find a support you may fall back down to the start but still climb back up on what you have already produced previously.

If you can produce strong attachments and contacts as you move upwards you can reach extremes very much like rainforest rattan stems which can get to over 150 metres using their hooked attachments. Some are knotted forming circular hoops, others may twist like corkscrews around trees. Others form monkey ladders which hang down from trees and help to anchor other plants. Once reaching the canopy like you they flourish with an opportunity for expansion and put out tendrils to hold the main stem. You must first gain mastery and take the longer view if you want to get all the way to the top. Many of those who have gained overnight success have worked and climbed for many years to get to that point. This success can arrive sooner than you think, so you need to build up your energy to plot your path forward.

Some hemi-epiphytes are already at a certain stage in their surroundings but still let down long rope like roots to reach the ground and burrow into the soil to get support for more development.

3 ARE YOU A CLINGER OR A CLIMBER?

Do you often need to form secure roots for attachments as you reach for success?

Some plants, like ivy, produce roots or claspers from their stem which excrete a glue which fixes the stem to any shape or kind of surface. By doing this you can ensure a safe, firm basis for further growth. Using this method, you can go really high like ivy, some vines or hydrangeas. These can travel miles upwards on rocks, houses and trees if allowed. Some plants are experts. It doesn't matter if you're smart or ambitious you need time to build up your skills first. Many people want to get to the top as fast as possible, but however furious you approach this you need strength especially at the foundation stage, and it takes time to achieve that.

When you want to get to the top fast, but have neglected to build a sturdy base, you turn into the second-class climber/business type. Those who reach their full potential know that what they are doing is right and have a good eye for detail. They have great drive for the duration of their progress giving all to their tasks.

4 ARE YOU A TWINER BUT USING TENDRILS FOR ATTACHMENTS?

Do you try to bring other opportunities that increases closer links to start to climb?

Stem tendrils in plants are able to grasp almost anything if contacted. Many plants, such as vines and passion flowers, produce opportunistic tendrils. Once attached they can support a great weight and have a strong pulling force. Once the contact is made the tendril spirals around the objective and the rest of the tendril twists up like a spring or old telephone cord. One half in one direction and the other half in the other. This spring tightens, dragging what it wants nearer to it and then strengthens and thickens so as to form a strong attachment. Like tendrils you have learnt how best to deal with everyday pressures and created a coping mechanism which works best for you. They also know that adversity builds character and have learnt how to deal with demanding situations, embracing the outer limits of their potential. Rather than avoiding pressure they feel challenged by it, and remain calm and relaxed under fire instead of surrendering to panic.

To be this sort of person you must react to even the slight stimulation or inkling of an opportunity. Plant tendrils can be as long as 40cm and react within 25 seconds, but many take a few hours to start capturing their opportunity of a secure position helping them to get to a higher position.

The tendrils can sweep around looking for opportunity in all sorts of paths ranging from circular to pendulum or even zig zag often following the sun. They may start to coil and even if there is no contact but will uncoil to try again. You need to purposely continue moving, zig-zagging up and down and sideways. The greater the energy behind this purpose then the increased focus and improved quality will bring you closer to achievement.

Tendrils are often found in fast growing plants so you will have to be someone constantly on the lookout for opportunities. These attachments are firm and no amount of wind or disturbance will dislodge them. Tendril activity is a kind of reflex which occurs during the day and night so you may have to also be a night owl. You have that reason to work when others sleep. You may have to temporarily sacrifice a safe life for a risky one with no ceiling. Find it by asking why, and not stopping until you hit your core. Examine the emotional reasons for wanting to change your status, or the status of others. Tendrils get stronger with age as the forces on the main stem become higher. Some tendrils avoid light and look for crevices, some tendrils are weaker than others, and some can produce more than 30 turns when coiled. They can be habituated by touching other tendrils or by rain drops.

Some tendrils can have adhesive pads at the end like Virginia Creeper and some begnonias and vetches. Make sure your ideas and links stick giving permanent supports on the way up.

5 ARE YOU A TWINER WHERE YOU USE EXTERNAL PARTS TO MAKE CONTACT?

In plants, these tendrils are part or all of the leaves being most sensitive when young and maybe on both sides as sweet peas and clematis. There may be a hook at the end of the leaf and it bends towards the side that is touched. Once an object is clasped it won't release. This is a steady step by step process you need to keep going.

The odd failure caused by taking risks and stretching yourself beyond what you think you can achieve is good. By taking risks, you truly will see the rewards You may need to give up unpromising directions of growth but you can bounce back many times with resilience and have future opportunities for success. There is a need to get rid of everything that is not linked to your goals and has a negative effect on your business. Like plants adapt, change and evolve but never, never quit.

MIKE PEARCE

Some advice for prospective climbers

- **LOOK OUT FOR COMPETITORS IN THE SAME AREAS**

- **MAINTAIN HIGH CONTACT WITH CUSTOMERS.**

- **IDENTIFY THE LEAST SPECIALISED AND FLEXIBLE WHO CAN CARRY OUT MOST FUNCTIONS. THESE HAVE THE ABILITY TO DIFFERENTIATE INTO OTHER ROLES UNDER SPECIAL CONDITIONS ESPECIALLY WHEN SOMETHING GOES WRONG.**

- **IDENTIFY THOSE WHO ARE STRONGER, MORE MATURE AND CAN FORM THE STRINGS OF THE ORGANISATION WITH A ROLE IN SUPPORT.**

- IDENTIFY THOSE WHO ARE AT THEIR LEVEL AND ARE IMPORTANT STRUCTURALLY BUT MAY NOT PROGRESS FURTHER.

- IDENTIFY THOSE WHO WILL FORM THE MAIN BULK OF THE ORGANISATION.

- NEW EMPLOYEES CAN THRIVE BUT FOR OTHERS THE HABITAT WILL BE UNFAVOURABLE AND THEY MAY LEAVE.

- NEED TO LOOK FOR SIMILAR OVERLAPPING. ACTIVITIES IN DIFFERENT DEPARTMENTS WHICH COULD BE SLOWING THE FLOW AND PRODUCE BOTTLE NECKS AND REDUCE THE RANGE OF TASKS IF POSSIBLE.

- BE AWARE THAT SOME BUSINESSES WILL REMAIN HIDDEN UNDER THE EARTH WAITING FOR THE RIGHT MOMENT TO EMERGE

- A TRIGGER MAY CAUSE SUCKERS TO DEVELOP ON THE ROOTS OF THE BUSINESS TO TAKE IN MORE SUPPLIES TO HELP GROWTH.

- AVOID GROWING TOO BIG TOO FAST SO AS NOT TO RUN OUT OF RESOURCES.

- ACCURATELY POSITION YOURSELF SO AS TO GET MAXIMUM EXPOSURE AND BE ABLE TO SPREAD

- REMEMBER YOU MAY REACH GREAT HEIGHTS BUT STILL NOT DOMINATE.

- ENSURE OFF SHOOTS HAVE THEIR OWN SUPPLIES.

- TRAIN YOUR MAIN STEM OF BUSINESS TO ENSURE DIRECTION IS MAINTAINED. SUCCESS DEPENDS ON THE TYPES OF PATTERNS PRODUCED

- BEWARE OF THOSE UNKNOWN WORKING IN THE SHADE.

- NOTE THERE ARE CONSTANTS LIKE OVERALL SHAPE AND BRANCHING OUT PATTERNS, BUT YOU MAY NOT BE ABLE TO PREDICT WHERE A NEW BRANCH WILL EMERGE.

- THE CUTTING EDGE OR TIPS OF YOUR BUSINESS WILL BE WHERE A GROWTH DIRECTION CAN OCCUR. THIS IS PRIMARY GROWTH.

- SECONDARY GROWTH INVOLVES ENLARGING PARTS OF THE ORGANISATION ALREADY FUNCTIONING. THIS MUST BE WELL DESIGNED AND ENSURE THAT EACH SECTION IS ROBUST, WITHIN THE REMIT OF THE ORGANISATION AND INCLUDES GOOD CUSTOMER AWARENESS AND COST EFFECTIVENESS.

- **BE AWARE THAT THE INFLUENCE OF LIGHT LEVELS, TEMPERATURE, HUMIDITY AND VENTILATION CAN AFFECT THE BEHAVIOUR AND PERFORMANCE OF STAFF.**

- **THE PRESENCE OF WATER AS DRINKS DISPENSERS CAN POSITIVELY CONTRIBUTE MENTALLY AND PHYSICALLY TOWARDS TASK ACHIEVEMENT.**

- **ENSURE YOU ARE AWARE OF THE FINE BALANCE THAT EXISTS WHICH MAY BE INFLUENCED BY THE SLIGHTEST CHANGE IN A SINGLE FACTO**

- NOTE AS WITH PLANTS, STAFF OR PRODUCTS IN ISOLATION TEND TO BE ATTACKED MORE.

- PARTNERSHIPS CAN HELP PROTECT AGAINST DISASTERS, IDENTIFY PRIORITIES AND ALLOW DIFFERENT CONTRIBUTIONS TO ACHIEVE A COMMON GOAL.

- LARGE BUSINESSES NEED TO PRE-EMPT COMPETITION AND NEED CAPACITY AGAINST RISKS TAKEN.

- SYSTEMS ARE NOT STATIC AND THERE ARE ALWAYS CHANGES GOING ON SO AS A MANAGER YOU NEED TO BE TOUGH AND ACCOMMODATING.

- SOME KINDS OF BUSINESS, THEIR ENVIRONMENT AND LOCALITY MAY BE SUBJECT TO HIGHER COMPETITION AND THEREFORE MORE SUSCEPTIBLE.

- ENSURE NO OTHER COMPANY IS FEEDING UNNOTICED ON YOUR BUSINESS.

- YOUR BUSINESS MUST DEVELOP DEFENCE LIKE THICK SPINES AND THICK SKIN NEARER THE OUTSIDE.

- ENSURE THAT TOO MUCH OVER GROWTH DOES NOT PUT YOUR HEAD OVER THE PARAPET AND INCREASE VULNERABILITY.

- COMPETITION MAY BE SUPERFICIAL OR DEEP ATTACK.

- **REDUCED SPACE, FLEXIBILITY AND POOR USE OF HUMAN RESOURCES CAN MAKE YOU VULNERABLE**

- **LOOK FOR NICHES OR DEEP CRACKS IN OTHER BUSINESSES WHERE YOUR BUSINESS COULD GROW.**

- **LOOK TO COLONISING NEW TERRITORIES AND EVOLVING DIFFERENT FORMS.**

- **THE MORE SPECIALISMS YOU DEVELOP THE TIGHTER METHODS THAT CAN BE USED FOR WORKER PRODUCTIVITY.**

- **YOU NEED TO DEPEND ON INITIAL FRAME WORKS WHERE UNIFORMITY IS CRUCIAL TO BUILD ON**

- **THE MORE VIGOROUS TYPES ADAPT, EVOLVE MORE WITH NEW METHODS TO FACE NEW OR DIFFICULT CHALLENGES WHICH CAN MAKE THEM SUCCESSFUL.**

- **INVASIVE ALIENS ARE OFTEN HOSTILE.**

- **SOME INVADERS HAVE DIFFERENT DEGREES OF TOXICITY AND THEIR EFFECTS CAN INCREASE THROUGH TIME OR BY CERTAIN ACTIONS.**

- **BE LIKE THE MOST AGGRESSIVE BRAMBLES WAVING YOUR SHOOTS, THRUSTING AHEAD RELENTLESSLY. CLIMB OVER ANYTHING IN THE WAY AND PROTECT YOURSELF WITH SPINES AS YOU DO THIS**

- **ENERGY IS NEEDED TO STIMULATE RAPID CLIMBING IN BUSINESS. SOMETIMES THIS IS EXPLOSIVE.**

- **BIG BUSINESSES LIKE LARGE CLIMBERS CAN SPREAD THEIR INFLUENCE FURTHER.**

- **NOTE SOME FRUITS OF BUSINESS MAY RIPEN AT DIFFERENT TIMES ATTRACTING DIFFERENT CUSTOMERS OR OPPORTUNITIES.**

- **RESOURCES MAY BE WITHDRAWN IN SOME CONDITIONS SO THAT ORGANISATIONS HAVE TO DEPEND ON WHAT HAS BEEN BUILT UP AND STORED.**

- **IDENTIFY THOSE PEOPLE THAT REMAIN DORMANT MENTALLY AND PHYSIOLOGICALLY. THESE CAN STAND UP TO VIGOROUS CONDITIONS AND CAN COME OUT OF THE WORST CATASTROPHES UNSCATHED.**

- **SOME ORGANISATIONS CAN THRIVE IN AREAS OF DISTURBANCE WITH OTHERS.**

- **YOU NEED TO KNOW THE SERIES OF SLOW CHANGES WHICH COULD CONTRIBUTE TO A LARGER DYNAMIC CHANGE.**

- **EXPANSION CAN OCCUR IN SMALL CREVICES WHERE A FOOTHOLD IS GAINED. THESE CAN INFLUENCE AND PENETRATE DEEP INTO FOUNDATIONS OF THE BUSINESS.**

- SOME BUSINESSES CAN FEND FOR THEMSELVES WITHOUT CONSTANT ATTENTION BUT MAY TAKE YEARS TO FILL THE GAPS.

- USING SUPPORT CAN ALSO HELP COMPETITORS BRINGING THEM CLOSER TO SIMILAR AREAS OF WORK

- GROWTH CAN BE MORE RESTRICTED IN A RESTRICTED ENVIRONMENT.

- REPEATING THE SAME WORKING APPROACH FOR SEVERAL YEARS MAY NOT TAKE INTO ACCOUNT TRENDING AND SIDELINES.

- **WITH STRATIFICATION YOU NEED TO ENSURE LOWER LEVELS ARE MORE FERTILE AND CAN ACTUALLY PUT PROCESSES INTO PLACE.**

- **CULTURE AND CLIMATE AFFECTS NATURE OF STAFF AND HASTENS OR SLOWS DOWN PROGRESS AND REPONSIVENESS.**

- **LOOK AT EFFECTS OF DECENTRALISING OR MAKING MORE WIDESPREAD SERVICES BUT ENHANCING CUSTOMER CONTACT.**

- **CHANGE ENVIRONMENTS WHERE POOR AND ALLOW PLENTY OF SPACE.**

- **ENSURE YOUR ENVIRONMENT SUPPORTS TALL GROWTH AND STABILITY ANCHORED AT BASE**

- YOU MUST BE FLEXIBLE AND USE TRIAL AND ERROR SO AS TO ELIMINATE WASTED TIME.

- WORK OUT CRITICAL PATHS, BEING LONGEST PATHS OF ACTIVITIES FROM START TO FINISH AND ADJUST.

- CHANCE PLAYS A PART IN INITIAL STAFF SELECTION BUT SELECTION AND ROLE IS TIGHTENED AS AN ORGANISATION GROWS.

- SURVIVAL DEPENDS ON THE ABILITY TO TOLERATE THE CONDITIONS IN THE HABITAT BUT THESE COULD STILL CHANGE.

- ADJACENT STAFF CAN AFFECT PERFORMANCE AND CHANGES MAY NEED TO BE MADE.

MIKE PEARCE

- **YOU MAY NEED ANNUAL CUTBACKS TO HELP IMPROVE YIELD AND QUALITY.**

To see other publications below by the author visit
snappysnappybooks.com

The really, really, really useful series

How to be a Successful Business Weed
How to Deal with Life's Snakes and Ladders
Know Your Students and Build Your Image
Pens for Pops
How to be a Successful Charity Shop
Make up-revealed
Ronnie's Sermon snippets
Wastefulness-Bone and Urine
Fertility Stones and Chocolate Eggs

Other books by Mike Pearce:

Pattern for Purpose- God's and Man's designs
Red Fred Cell and Friends
Human Termites eat London
Pigeons Splat London
Glass Anemones Tentacle-ize London
Tuppeny Hangover
I am Termite
The littlest Oyster
Bits and Bobs
The Shell Man
Cats at Christmas
Tails, Tales
Trust-Nothing but a Must
In a Dark, Dark Corner was the Holy Ghost
The Shell Lady
Captain Grottbuster versus the Grey World
London's Nemesis (Trilogy of 3, 4 and 5 above
Saved by Angels (Trilogy of 6, 8 and 14 above)
The World of Wax

Photosynthetic Women
Queen Rat on Deadman's Island
The Watcher on the Fal
The Rock Pool
The Little Shepherd Boy's Gift
The Living Fossils
Old Mother Nature Laughed and Laughed
Betty's Barcodes
Time Runs Dry (play)
Valentines Cards
The Scrofula Infirmary
The Cornish Urchin
My Therizinosaurus
Spider in the Tomb
The White Cockerel
The Red Church Doll
Butterfly Angels (compilation of previous books)
The Girl Under the Paeony Tree
Baby Feet
The Sparrows' Last Soul
I Herring Gull
Ball Rooms

ABOUT THE AUTHOR

Dr Mike Pearce is a scientist interested in behaviour. He also was a lecturer in human biology and health at a college in Canterbury, Kent.